Who  By Here?

Lada Kratky

Illustrated by Katey Monaghan

HAMPTON-BROWN BOOKS
MANY CULTURES, MANY LANGUAGES...MANY POSSIBILITIES!™

Who came by here?
A hen came by.

Who came by here?

A horse came by.

Who came by here?

A duck came by.

Who came by here?

Uh-oh! Bad dog!